Allergy-Free
recipes for Kids

Publications International, Ltd.

Recipe development on pages 30, 36, 42, 44, 48, 66, 70, 74, 86, 88, 90, 94, 120, 122 and 134 by Bev Bennett.
Recipe Development on pages 32, 54, 124, 128, 130 and 136 by Marilyn Pocius.

Photography on pages 27, 31, 33, 35, 37, 43, 45, 49, 55, 65, 67, 71, 73, 75, 87, 89, 91, 95, 113, 119, 121, 123, 125, 129, 131, 135 and 137 by PIL Photo Studio, Chicago.
Photographer: Annemarie Zelasko
Photographer's Assistant: Tony Favarula
Food Stylists: Kathy Aragaki, Carol Smoler
Assistant Food Stylists: Sara Cruz, Lissa Levy

Pictured on the front cover *(clockwise from top right):* Corny Critters *(page 16),* Suzie's Sloppy Joes *(page 38),* Allergy-Free Mac & Cheez *(page 32)* and Fudge Mini Cupcakes *(page 30).*
Pictured on the back cover *(left to right):* Chicken & Sweet Potato Chili *(page 62)* and Blueberry Pancake Smiles *(page 12).*

Contributing Writer: Marilyn Pocius

ISBN-13: 978-1-4508-3773-6
ISBN-10: 1-4508-3773-5

Library of Congress Control Number: 2011937419

Manufactured in China.

8 7 6 5 4 3 2 1

Microwave Cooking: Microwave ovens vary in wattage. Use the cooking times as guidelines and check for doneness before adding more time.

pil Publications International, Ltd.

contents

allergy-free cooking for kids

It is estimated that more than 11 million people have food allergies. According to the Centers for Disease Control and Prevention, the number of children allergic to foods has increased 18 percent in the last decade. There are many theories, but no proven explanations for this increase. The good news is that a great deal of research is underway and awareness has increased everywhere from school to the doctor's office.

What Is a Food Allergy?

The term "food allergy" means different things to different people. By definition, a true allergy is one in which the body's immune system overreacts to a protein that is normally harmless. Symptoms can range from a rash to anaphylactic shock. Milk, egg and nut allergies are classic examples. Food sensitivities or intolerances are often also called allergies, though they don't fit the same narrow definition. For example, many people are sensitive to the lactose in milk products and have trouble digesting it. Strictly speaking, they are lactose intolerant, not allergic to dairy. Those with celiac disease have an autoimmune condition caused by a reaction to the gluten in food. It is a serious, chronic condition, not a true allergy.

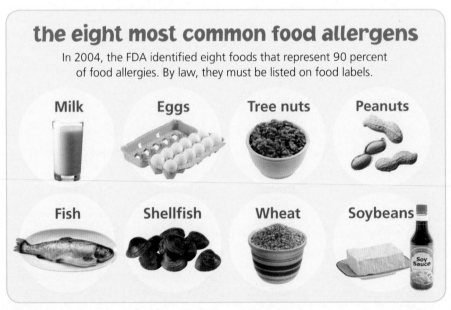

the eight most common food allergens

In 2004, the FDA identified eight foods that represent 90 percent of food allergies. By law, they must be listed on food labels.

Milk   Eggs   Tree nuts   Peanuts

Fish   Shellfish   Wheat   Soybeans

Note: *This book does not specifically label recipes that are free of fish and shellfish since none of the recipes contain these allergens.*

How to Use This Book

The recipes in this book were chosen to offer a variety of good tasting, kid friendly food that is free from some, but not necessarily all, of the eight most common food allergens. The icons for each recipe will give you a quick idea of which allergens are missing and which recipes may be right for your child. There are no recipes that use fish or shellfish as ingredients.

You and your doctor are the best judges of what is appropriate for your child. If he or she is very sensitive be careful of ingredients that are free of allergens but are processed in a facility that also handles foods that are made with them. It is also vital to check labels every time you purchase a product since ingredients change and even something that you've used before without problems may no longer be safe.

Variations to the recipes are given where appropriate. For instance, if cheese or other dairy products can be eliminated, a dairy-free option is included under the main recipe.

Always have your doctor evaluate your child's allergies. Misinterpreting symptoms or self-diagnosing can be very dangerous.

the icons and their meaning

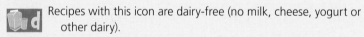
Recipes with this icon are dairy-free (no milk, cheese, yogurt or other dairy).

Recipes with this icon contain no eggs or egg products.

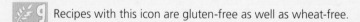
Recipes with this icon are gluten-free as well as wheat-free.

Recipes with this icon contain no tree nuts or coconut.

Recipes with this icon contain no peanuts or peanut products.

Recipes with this icon contain no soy or soy products.

cooking dairy-free and easy

Two Kinds of Sensitivity

1. Lactose Intolerance

Lactose is the natural sugar in milk. Many people don't produce enough of the enzyme lactase to properly digest lactose. Since there is lactose present in breast milk, virtually all babies can digest it without problems. Lactose intolerance usually shows up after age five when the amount of the needed enzyme may diminish. Symptoms of lactose intolerance include stomach pain or diarrhea. Cheese and butter tend to be lower in lactose than milk, so may be tolerated. Lactose-free milk is also available. Consult your physician if you suspect your child is lactose sensitive.

2. Milk Allergy

As with other true allergies, being allergic to cow's milk means that the immune system overreacts to a protein—usually casein or whey. Symptoms of a milk allergy can be mild or as severe and life-threatening as anaphylactic shock. Children with a milk allergy must avoid all dairy in any form.

Be a Label Detective

Did you know that most margarine contains dairy? Are you aware that hydrolyzed casein and whey powder are dairy products? Fortunately, U.S. food manufacturers are now required to list the simple word "milk" as part of the ingredient list or in boldface type at the end of the list, even if the actual ingredient goes by an obscure chemical name. The recent popularity of the vegan diet is a boon for the dairy-free shopper, too. Since vegans consume no animal products, you can assume products labeled vegan are dairy-free. The kosher designation "pareve" is another handy indicator that the product contains no milk.

Non-Dairy is NOT always Dairy-Free

Many products labeled non-dairy contain whey, casein or other milk-derived ingredients. According to the FDA, non-dairy products can contain 0.5 percent or less of milk products by weight. Non-dairy creamers and non-dairy whipped toppings usually contain dairy in some form.

understanding wheat and gluten

Gluten is a protein found naturally in wheat, rye and barley. Those with a sensitivity to gluten must avoid all three grains as well as any products that use gluten as an ingredient. A wheat allergy is similar to a gluten allergy, but instead of avoiding all gluten-containing foods, you must only avoid wheat. Celiac disease is often called a gluten allergy, but it is actually an autoimmune reaction to gluten and is a serious, chronic condition, not an allergy. Your child may grow out of a wheat allergy, but not celiac disease. In this book, recipes with the G icon are both wheat and gluten-free.

Eliminating gluten from the food we eat is a lot more complicated than eliminating bread. There is gluten in most of kids' favorite foods—pasta, crackers, bagels, pretzels, pizza, donuts and even chicken nuggets. The good news is that there are many more foods on the gluten-free list than on the forbidden one. There are also more products, from cereals to baking mixes to pastas, that are now being formulated in gluten-free versions. Eating gluten-free can also mean a healthier diet with more fruits and vegetables and less processed food.

dairy-free and gluten-free: the GFCF diet

Many families are choosing a gluten-free casein-free (GFCF) diet for children with symptoms of ADD/ADHD or autism. While there is no scientific evidence that eliminating gluten and casein helps these conditions, there are many anecdotal accounts of improvements in symptoms. Why would this be so? One theory is that some children are not able to completely digest the protein in milk (casein) and wheat (gluten) and that these leftover proteins form peptides in the blood that act like opiates in the body, influencing behavior. Research in the U.S. and Europe has found peptides in the urine of a significant number of children with autism.

Studies are currently underway to see if the GFCF diet really can be proven effective. Always consult your doctor before changing your child's diet. Tests can determine sensitivities to gluten and casein and whether there are peptides present. You should also get professional dietary advice to ensure your child will be getting the nutrition he or she needs.

Introduction  7

egg allergies, unscrambled

Egg allergies usually occur in early childhood and more than half of those are outgrown by age seven. Of course, as with all allergies, there are exceptions. In some cases, the allergy remains lifelong or first surfaces in adolescence or adulthood. Both the yolk and the white of an egg contain proteins that can cause a reaction.

An Egg by Any Other Name

At first blush, avoiding eggs sounds simple. Just don't serve them poached, scrambled, fried or over easy! Unfortunately, eggs are present in many foods and hide under many names. Most baked goods use eggs for richness and lightness and the shiny crust on breads and pastries is created with an egg wash. Commercially made pancakes, waffles, donuts, crackers and pretzels usually contain eggs, as do many sauces and prepared entrées. Chances are most food that is battered or breaded also contains egg, since it helps the coating stick. Pasta and noodles are usually made with eggs, but there are some egg-free versions available.

Label Lingo

You probably know that mayonnaise, meringue and custard must be avoided. You may not know that there are some obscure ingredient names that are aliases for eggs. Any word beginning with the prefix "ovo" is suspicious. Albumin and globulin are also egg products. Always read labels carefully and check for the allergen statement, which legally must appear somewhere.

Baking without Cracking an Egg

In many baked goods requiring no more than three eggs, silken tofu is an acceptable replacement. (Use ¼ cup of tofu to replace each egg.) One mashed banana or ¼ cup of applesauce can often fill in for one egg in quick breads or muffins that are on the sweet side. One tablespoon ground flaxseed mixed with 2 tablespoons water can also be used in place of one egg. Commercial powdered egg replacer is another option. Follow the package directions and mix it with water before use.

When Is an Egg Substitute NOT a Substitute?

Most cholesterol-free egg substitutes are made from egg whites. They were created to allow people to enjoy eggs without the cholesterol found in the yolks. There are a few egg-free replacement products available, like egg-free mayonnaise, but check labels carefully. Look for one that specifies "vegan."

  Introduction

nut allergies in a nutshell

Tree Nuts and Peanuts

Both tree nuts and peanuts are frequent allergens for children. You are probably aware that peanuts are legumes, not nuts. You may also know that many children and adults who are allergic to peanuts are also allergic to tree nuts and vice versa.

It's Nuts Not to Be Cautious

While very few reactions are severe, even a mild allergic response to nuts should be taken seriously. Future reactions can be more troublesome. Peanut allergy is responsible for more fatalities than any other food allergy. Even trace amounts can cause reactions.

Tree nuts include almonds, Brazil nuts, cashews, filberts (hazelnuts), macadamia nuts, pecans, pine nuts (pignoli), pistachios and walnuts. A person may be allergic to only one or two tree nuts, but it's best to avoid them all unless you are certain.

A Nut by Any Other Name

Nut proteins can be present in candies, cookies, crackers and other processed foods. Peanut oil is frequently used for cooking, especially in Asian and other ethnic recipes. Read labels carefully every time. Don't assume that ingredients haven't changed—they often do. Be aware that highly refined peanut oil is NOT required by the FDA to be listed on ingredients panels. Refining removes the protein and studied have found that this eliminates most allergic reactions.

When Is a Nut Not a Nut?

When it's a water chestnut or a nutmeg. Neither is botanically related to tree nuts or peanuts, so they rarely present a problem. Coconut is a fruit and is usually not allergenic. However, the FDA recently reclassified it as a tree nut, so products that contain coconut now carry a warning and carry the nut icon in this book. Pine nuts are also considered tree nuts, but are sometimes tolerated. Soy nuts are legumes, not nuts. Consult your doctor and when in doubt, don't!

Some Nutty Substitutions

Nuts used as a topping can easily be replaced with crushed potato chips, corn chips or toasted bread crumbs. Sunflower or pumpkin seeds can be excellent nut replacements, if they are tolerated. Sunflower seed butter or soy nut butter can stand in for peanut butter.

sneaky soy hides in many places

An allergy to soy is one of the most common in children. Soybeans are legumes like peanuts, so if one is an allergen often both are. Soy can be found everywhere—from bread and meat to ice cream and French fries. In fact, one of the most difficult parts of dealing with a soy allergy is spotting the hidden soy in processed foods. Take our Soy Spotter Quiz for some surprises.

soy spotter quiz
Which of these foods may contain soy?

| 1 Chocolate Chips | 2 Seitan | 3 Chicken Broth | 4 Pasta Sauce |
| 5 Vegetable Oil | 6 Edamame | 7 Cooking Spray | 8 Tofu |

ANSWERS: All of the above! Numbers 2, 6 and 8 are made from soybeans. All other items may contain soy in some form.

Soy also lurks in snack foods, like chips and crackers, and in baked goods often in the form of soy flour. Many, in fact most, dairy-free cheeses, margarines, yogurts and spreads are made with soy. It can be used in salad dressings, boxed dinners and even vitamin pills and lip balm. Chocolate chips and chocolate candy almost always contains soy lecithin. Fortunately, if soy is part of a food product in any form (with one exception, see the next paragraph), by law it must be listed as in ingredient. In other words, if hydrolyzed vegetable protein is made from soy, the label will say so.

The Exception to the Rule

Highly refined soybean oil is NOT considered an allergen and does not have to be listed as an ingredient. This form of soy has been treated (neutralized, bleached and deodorized) and contains very low levels of proteins, which are the typical soy allergens. Soy oil that is NOT highly refined, but instead is cold pressed, expeller pressed or extruded does NOT fall into this category and is not safe.

happy, healthy allergy-free kids

How do you explain to your child that he or she can't have a piece of Johnny's birthday cake or that those chocolate chip cookies that smell so good are off limits? It sounds impossible. Most parents would much rather make sacrifices themselves than ask their children to make them. Kids are, fortunately, considerably more resilient than we think and an allergy-free lifestyle has positive benefits even from a pint-size perspective. Chances are this change in diet is going to be a lot harder on you than on your child.

tips to ease the way

1. Give Them Control. The more your child understands his or her dietary restrictions and the reasons for them, the better. Sooner or later he will have to make decisions when you're not around.

2. Spread the Word. Make baby-sitters, friends' parents, relatives and school officials aware that your child is allergic to certain foods and that it is extremely important he avoids them.

3. Home Work. Keep your kitchen safe from cross-contamination by eliminating any known allergens. Make it easy for your child to find delicious and nutritious snacks.

4. Party Plan. If your son or daughter is invited to a birthday party or sleepover, send along replacements for whatever is being served. Explain the situation to the parent in charge and let them know what you're sending.

5. Find Alternatives. You will not be able to replace chocolate ice cream with broccoli. Instead make Intense Chocolate Ice Cream (page 36) or another safe treat.

6. Lunch Breaks. What lunch looks like is important. Other kids can be mean and make fun of food that looks different. Consult with your child for help in creating a safe but "cool" lunch.

7. Don't Make it a Big Deal. It is a big deal for you, but a kid's world is filled with friends, pets, bikes, superheroes and recess. They are probably not obsessing about food like you are, and that's good.

Start Right

blueberry pancake smiles

½ cup sorghum flour
¼ cup brown rice flour
¼ cup buckwheat flour*
2 tablespoons sugar
2 teaspoons baking powder
⅛ teaspoon xanthan gum
1 to 1¼ cups rice milk
Prepared powdered egg replacer equal to 1 egg
2 tablespoons vegetable oil
1 cup blueberries
Maple syrup

Despite its name, there is no wheat or gluten in buckwheat. It's related to rhubarb.

1. Combine sorghum flour, brown rice flour, buckwheat flour, sugar, baking powder and xanthan gum in medium bowl. Whisk in 1 cup rice milk, egg replacer and oil until ingredients are moistened, adding additional rice milk if needed.

2. Spray large skillet with nonstick cooking spray. Heat over medium heat. Spoon batter into skillet 1 tablespoon at a time. Arrange blueberries on batter to make funny faces. Cook until bubbles cover surface of pancakes and bottoms are golden brown. Turn and cook 1 minute or until lightly browned.

Makes about 16 small pancakes

breakfast burgers

 free from

¾ pound extra-lean ground turkey
½ cup minced red bell pepper
½ cup minced green bell pepper
2 teaspoons dried onion flakes
1 teaspoon dried parsley flakes
½ teaspoon black pepper
Nonstick cooking spray
4 whole wheat English muffins
4 large spinach leaves
4 slices cheese

1. Mix turkey, bell peppers, onion flakes, parsley and black pepper in large bowl. Shape mixture into four patties; spray with cooking spray.

2. Cook patties in large nonstick skillet over medium heat 7 minutes or until lightly browned on bottom. Turn and cook 7 minutes more. Add 2 tablespoons water; cover and cook 3 minutes or until cooked through (165°F).

3. Toast English muffins. Place one spinach leaf, one turkey burger and one slice cheese on each muffin half; top with remaining muffin half. *Makes 4 servings*

dairy-free gluten-free variation: Omit cheese and muffins. Serve with tomato slices and condiments or on dairy-free gluten-free bread or buns.

melon cup

 free from

2 cups cubed watermelon (or any melon)
3 cups vanilla dairy-free soy-free yogurt
½ cup natural granola

Place melon in four bowls. Top with yogurt and granola. *Makes 4 servings*

gluten-free variation: Replace granola with any gluten-free cereal.

cherry-orange oatmeal

1 can (11 ounces) mandarin orange segments in light syrup, drained, divided
1 cup fresh pitted cherries or frozen dark sweet cherries, divided
2 cups water
1 cup gluten-free oats
2 tablespoons sugar
1 tablespoon unsweetened cocoa powder

1. Set aside eight orange segments and four cherries for garnish.

2. Combine water, remaining orange segments and cherries, oats, sugar and cocoa in medium microwavable bowl. Microwave on HIGH 2 minutes. Stir; microwave 4 minutes.

3. Divide mixture evenly among four serving bowls. Garnish with reserved oranges and cherries.

Makes 4 servings

> Oats have been off and on the gluten-free list for years. The main problem is that most regular oats are processed in facilities that also handle wheat products and are contaminated for that reason. There are now many brands of certified gluten-free oats available that are safe for most everyone. There does seem to be a very small subset of gluten-sensitive people who have a problem with a protein present in oats of any kind. Research is still underway.

spiced sweet potato muffins

 free from d e g n p s

½ cup plus 2 tablespoons packed brown sugar, divided
2 teaspoons ground cinnamon, divided
1½ cups Gluten-Free All-Purpose Flour Blend (recipe follows)
1 tablespoon baking powder
½ teaspoon salt
½ teaspoon baking soda
½ teaspoon ground allspice
½ teaspoon xanthan gum
1 cup mashed cooked or canned sweet potatoes
¾ cup rice milk
¼ cup vegetable oil
¼ cup unsweetened applesauce

1. Preheat oven to 425°F. Grease 12 standard (2½-inch) muffin cups. Combine 2 tablespoons brown sugar and 1 teaspoon cinnamon in small bowl.

2. Combine flour blend, baking powder, remaining 1 teaspoon cinnamon, salt, baking soda, allspice and xanthan gum in large bowl. Stir in remaining ⅓ cup brown sugar.

3. Combine sweet potatoes, rice milk, oil and applesauce in medium bowl. Stir into flour mixture just until moistened. Spoon evenly into prepared muffin cups. Sprinkle with cinnamon mixture.

4. Bake 14 to 16 minutes or until toothpick inserted into centers comes out clean. Remove to wire rack; cool completely.   *Makes 12 muffins*

gluten-free all-purpose flour blend: Combine 1 cup white rice flour, 1 cup sorghum flour, 1 cup tapioca flour, 1 cup cornstarch and 1 cup quinoa flour in large bowl. Whisk to make sure flours are evenly distributed. The recipe can be doubled or tripled. Store in airtight container in the refrigerator. Makes about 5 cups.

note: If your child can tolerate nuts, try replacing quinoa flour in the flour blend with coconut or almond flour to add just a touch of sweetness.

corny critters

free from

- **1 cup cornmeal**
- **1 tablespoon sugar**
- **½ teaspoon salt**
- **1 cup boiling water**
- **½ cup Gluten-Free All-Purpose Flour Blend (page 16)**
- **½ cup rice milk**
- **1 egg, beaten**
- **2 tablespoons dairy-free soy-free margarine, melted**
- **2 teaspoons baking powder**
- **Dried apricots**
- **Sliced almonds**

1. Combine cornmeal, sugar and salt in medium bowl. Stir in boiling water. Cover; let stand 10 minutes.

2. Stir flour blend, rice milk, egg, margarine and baking powder into cornmeal until smooth.

3. Heat large nonstick skillet or griddle over medium heat. Brush lightly with oil. Transfer some of batter to measuring cup with pour spout. Cut apricots into shapes for noses, mouths and whiskers.

4. Pour small circles of batter onto skillet; drizzle additional batter to make puppy or bunny ears. Use a knife to straighten edges of batter as needed. Add almond eyes with dried cranberry pupils. Place pieces of dried apricot for noses and mouths. Press into batter.

5. Cook 2 to 3 minutes until bubbles appear on top of pancakes and edges become dull. Turn carefully with spatula sprayed with nonstick cooking spray. Cook 1 to 2 minutes until lightly browned on both sides. Serve pancakes with syrup or desired toppings. *Makes about 4 servings (10 to 12 pancakes)*

nut-free variation: Omit almonds.

fruity whole-grain cereal

 2 cups water
¼ cup quick-cooking pearled barley
¼ cup instant brown rice
¼ teaspoon salt
½ cup rice milk
⅓ cup golden raisins
¼ cup finely chopped dried pitted dates
¼ cup finely chopped dried plums
¼ cup quick oats
¼ cup oat bran
 2 tablespoons firmly packed brown sugar
½ teaspoon ground cinnamon

1. Combine water, barley, rice and salt in large saucepan. Bring to a boil over high heat. Reduce heat to low. Simmer, covered, 8 minutes or until rice and barley are soft but still slightly firm.

2. Stir in rice milk, raisins, dates, plums, oats, oat bran, brown sugar and cinnamon. Simmer, covered, 3 to 5 minutes or until cereal is creamy, stirring once.

3. Serve hot. Refrigerate any leftover cereal in airtight container.

Makes 6 (½-cup) servings

tip: To reheat, place one serving in microwavable bowl. Microwave 30 seconds; stir. Add water or rice milk for desired consistency. Microwave just until hot.

gluten-free variation: Replace barley with rice. Replace oats and oat bran with gluten-free oats.

potato-zucchini pancakes with warm corn salsa

Warm Corn Salsa (recipe follows)
2 cups frozen hash brown potatoes, thawed
1½ cups shredded zucchini, drained and squeezed dry
2 eggs, lightly beaten
¼ cup sweet rice flour (mochiko)
2 tablespoons chopped onion
2 tablespoons chopped green bell pepper
¼ teaspoon salt
⅛ teaspoon black pepper
1 to 2 tablespoons vegetable oil

1. Prepare Warm Corn Salsa; keep warm.

2. Combine potatoes, zucchini, eggs, rice flour, onion, bell pepper, salt and black pepper in medium bowl until well blended.

3. Heat 1 tablespoon oil in large nonstick skillet over medium-high heat. Drop potato mixture by ¼-cupfuls into skillet. Cook pancakes in batches about 3 minutes on each side or until golden brown, adding additional oil if needed. Serve with Warm Corn Salsa. *Makes 6 servings*

warm corn salsa

1 tablespoon olive oil
2 tablespoons chopped onion
2 tablespoons finely chopped green bell pepper
1 package (9 ounces) frozen corn, thawed
1 cup chunky salsa
2 teaspoons chopped fresh cilantro

Heat oil in large nonstick skillet. Add onion and bell pepper; cook and stir 3 minutes or until crisp tender. Add corn, salsa and cilantro. Reduce heat to medium-low; cook 5 minutes or until hot.

creamy fruit blend

1 medium banana, peeled and quartered
1 cup rice milk
1 small ripe peach, peeled, pitted and quartered
½ cup fresh or frozen unsweetened strawberries
½ cup white grape juice
2 tablespoons packed brown sugar
1 tablespoon lemon juice
½ teaspoon vanilla
   Fresh fruit (optional)

1. Combine banana, rice milk, peach, strawberries, grape juice, brown sugar, lemon juice and vanilla in blender. Blend until fruit is puréed and mixture is smooth.

2. Pour into two glasses. Garnish with fresh fruit. Serve immediately.

Makes 2 servings

variations: Other fruit can be substituted in this recipe. Try raspberries, blueberries, nectarines or pineapple for your own special combination. If fresh peaches are not available, you may substitute ⅔ cup frozen peach slices that have been partially thawed.

> Breakfast can be a challenging meal when you have to deal with allergies. Smoothies are an excellent solution that most kids love. For added nutrition, accompany the smoothie with a cereal that meets your child's dietary requirements.

apricot cranberry scones

2 cups Gluten-Free All-Purpose Flour Blend (page 16), plus additional for
  work surface
¼ cup sugar
2½ teaspoons baking powder
¾ teaspoon salt
¾ teaspoon xanthan gum
½ teaspoon baking soda
¼ cup chopped dried apricots
¼ cup dried cranberries
½ cup (1 stick) cold butter, cut into small pieces
½ cup plain yogurt
¾ cup milk

1. Preheat oven to 425°F.

2. Combine flour blend, sugar, baking powder, salt, xanthan gum and baking soda in large bowl. Add dried apricots and cranberries and toss to combine.

3. Cut butter into flour mixture with pastry blender or two knives until coarse crumbs form. Stir yogurt into milk in small bowl or large measuring cup until combined.

4. Gradually add wet ingredients to dry ingredients, stirring just until dough begins to form. (You may not need all of yogurt mixture.) Transfer to surface sprinkled with flour blend. Knead 5 or 6 times until dough clings together.

5. Pat dough into circle about ½ inch thick. Cut out 2-inch circles with floured biscuit cutter. Place 2 inches apart on baking sheet. Press together remaining dough and cut additional scones.

6. Bake 10 to 14 minutes or until lightly browned. Cool on wire rack.

Makes about 15 scones

sweet potato & sausage hash

 free from

4 ounces gluten-free Italian sausage
1 tablespoon vegetable oil
1 small red onion, finely chopped
1 small red bell pepper, finely chopped
1 small sweet potato, peeled and cut into ½-inch cubes
¼ teaspoon salt
¼ teaspoon black pepper
⅛ teaspoon cumin
⅛ teaspoon chipotle chili powder

1. Remove sausage from casings. Heat oil in large nonstick skillet over medium heat. Add sausage; cook and stir 3 minutes or until browned. Remove from skillet.

2. Add onion, bell pepper, sweet potato, salt, black pepper, cumin and chili powder to skillet. Cook and stir 5 to 8 minutes or until sweet potato is tender.

3. Stir in sausage; cook without stirring 5 minutes or until hash is lightly browned.

Makes 2 servings

Like most prepared foods, sausage can contain hidden allergens. Check labels carefully for wheat and soy, which are often used to improve texture or shelf life. One relatively easy option is to make your own sausage. After all, sausage is nothing more than ground meat with seasonings. For this recipe, ground turkey with Italian seasoning would be a fine substitute for prepared Italian sausage.

Kid Classics

fudge mini cupcakes

¾ cup allergen-free chocolate chips
3 tablespoons dairy-free soy-free margarine
3 eggs, separated
⅛ teaspoon salt
¼ cup granulated sugar
¼ cup powdered sugar

1. Preheat oven to 300°F. Line 12 mini (1¾-inch) muffin cups with paper baking cups.

2. Melt chocolate chips and margarine in top of double boiler over simmering water. Remove from heat; beat in egg yolks. Place egg whites and salt in large bowl. Beat with electric mixer at medium speed until foamy. Gradually add granulated sugar, beating until stiff peaks form. Fold chocolate mixture into egg whites.

3. Spoon batter into prepared muffin cups, filling two-thirds full. Bake 18 minutes or until cupcakes feel firm when very lightly touched. Cool in pan 5 minutes; remove to wire rack to cool completely. (Cupcakes will puff up, but then sink back.) Dust with powdered sugar before serving.

Makes about 3½ dozen cupcakes

allergy-free mac & cheez

cheez powder
- 2 tablespoons flaked nutritional yeast*
- 4 teaspoons sweet rice flour**
- ¾ teaspoon salt
- ½ teaspoon onion powder
- ½ teaspoon garlic powder
- ¼ teaspoon dry mustard

pasta
- 8 ounces uncooked gluten-free penne, rotini or other small pasta shape
- ½ cup rice milk

options
- Cooked chopped chicken or ground beef
- Cooked peas or carrot coins

Nutritional yeast can be found in health food stores and some supermarkets. It is NOT similar to regular yeast or brewer's yeast.

**Sweet rice flour is sometimes labeled glutinous rice flour (although it is gluten-free) or mochiko, the Japanese term. It is available in the Asian section of large supermarkets, at Asian grocers and online.*

1. Bring a large saucepan of water to a boil. Meanwhile, prepare cheez powder. Mix nutritional yeast, rice flour, salt, onion powder, garlic powder and mustard powder in small bowl until completely combined.*

2. Add pasta to boiling water and cook according to package directions until al dente. Reserve ½ cup pasta cooking water; drain pasta. Oil pasta lightly if needed to prevent sticking.

3. Stir cheez powder and rice milk in large saucepan until smooth. Add pasta; cook and stir over medium heat 1 to 2 minutes. Add 4 to 6 tablespoons pasta cooking water and continue cooking 2 minutes or until sauce coats pasta and desired consistency is reached. Stir in chicken, peas or carrots, if desired, and heat through.

Makes 4 servings

Cheez powder may be prepared in advance and stored in a covered container at room temperature. You may double or triple the quantities for future use. Use ¼ cup for 8 ounces of pasta.

wild west pizza

free from

3 cups Gluten-Free Flour Blend for Breads (recipe follows)
2 packages (¼ ounce each) active dry yeast
2 teaspoons xanthan gum
1 teaspoon salt
1¼ cups warm water
¼ cup extra virgin olive oil
3 egg whites
1 tablespoon honey
1 teaspoon cider vinegar

toppings
1½ cups gluten-free soy-free barbecue sauce
2 cups chopped cooked chicken
½ red onion, cut into thin slivers
1 bell pepper, finely chopped

1. Preheat oven to 450°F. Line baking sheets or pizza pans with parchment paper.

2. Mix flour blend, yeast, xanthan gum and salt in large bowl. Whisk 1 cup warm water, oil, egg whites, honey and vinegar in medium bowl. Beat wet ingredients into dry ingredients with electric mixer at low speed until combined. Add additional water by tablespoonfuls until batter is smooth and thick. Beat 5 minutes at medium-high speed, scraping bowl occasionally.

3. Transfer one third of dough to prepared baking sheets. Spread dough into 10-inch circle using dampened fingers or back of oiled spoon, making crust thicker around edge to hold toppings. Repeat with remaining dough.

4. Bake 8 to 10 minutes or until crusts are lightly browned.* Spread crusts with barbecue sauce. Top with chicken, onion slivers and bell pepper. Bake 2 to 5 minutes or until heated through.   *Makes 3 (10-inch) pizzas*

*To freeze pizza crusts for later use, allow them to cool, wrap well and store in the freezer for up to 3 months.

gluten-free flour blend for breads: Combine 1 cup brown rice flour, 1 cup sorghum flour, 1 cup tapioca flour, 1 cup cornstarch, ¾ cup millet flour or chickpea flour and ⅓ cup instant mashed potato flakes in large bowl. Whisk to make sure ingredients are evenly distributed. The recipe can be doubled or tripled. Store in airtight container in refrigerator.

intense chocolate ice cream

2 cups plain rice milk
¼ cup tapioca flour
¼ cup unsweetened cocoa powder
6 tablespoons granulated sugar
¼ teaspoon salt
½ teaspoon vanilla
⅓ cup allergen-free chocolate chips

1. Stir ½ cup rice milk, tapioca flour and cocoa in medium saucepan until smooth. Add remaining 1½ cups rice milk, sugar and salt. Cook over medium heat, stirring constantly, until mixture thickens to consistency of pudding. Remove from heat. Stir in vanilla and chocolate chips until chocolate melts.

2. Transfer to medium bowl. Cover and refrigerate 2 hours or until cold.

3. Pour mixture into ice cream maker and process according to manufacturer's directions.

Makes 4 servings

Top this decadent ice cream with fresh raspberries or other fruit. Or if you have the kind of kids who can never get enough chocolate, drizzle with chocolate syrup! Thankfully, cocoa and chocolate syrup are generally allergen-free. Chocolate chips often contain soy in the form of soy lecithin and many also include dairy products, although allergen-free brands are available. Read labels carefully.

suzie's sloppy joes

3 pounds lean ground beef
1 cup chopped onion
3 cloves garlic, minced
1¼ cups ketchup
1 cup chopped red bell pepper
¼ cup packed brown sugar
¼ cup water
3 tablespoons prepared mustard
3 tablespoons cider vinegar
2 teaspoons chili powder
Toasted hamburger buns

Slow Cooker Directions

1. Cook and stir ground beef, onion and garlic in large skillet 6 to 8 minutes over medium-high heat, stirring to separate beef. Drain fat.

2. Combine ketchup, bell pepper, brown sugar, water, mustard, vinegar and chili powder in slow cooker. Stir in beef mixture.

3. Cover; cook on LOW 6 to 8 hours. Serve on hamburger buns.

Makes 8 servings

gluten-free variation: Serve sloppy joes on gluten-free buns or over rice or quinoa.

extra crunchy chicken tenders

 free from

2 cups gluten-free corn flakes
1 cup gluten-free pretzels
½ teaspoon garlic powder
⅛ teaspoon paprika
⅛ teaspoon dry mustard
1 cup Gluten-Free All-Purpose Flour Blend (page 16)
1 teaspoon salt
½ teaspoon black pepper
3 eggs, lightly beaten
1 teaspoon gluten-free soy sauce
1 pound chicken tenders
Nonstick cooking spray
Gluten-free barbecue sauce or honey mustard (optional)

1. Preheat oven to 350°F. Combine corn flakes and pretzels in food processor; pulse until coarse crumbs form.

2. Pour crumbs in shallow dish; stir in garlic powder, paprika and mustard powder. Combine flour blend, salt and black pepper in another shallow dish. Combine eggs and soy sauce in third shallow dish.

3. Coat chicken with seasoned flour blend; shake off excess. Dip in egg mixture; drain. Transfer to crumb mixture; coat both sides with crumbs.

4. Spray large nonstick skillet with cooking spray. Working in batches, brown chicken on both sides; transfer to large baking sheet.

5. Bake 10 minutes or until chicken is cooked through. Serve with barbecue sauce or honey mustard for dipping. *Makes 4 to 6 servings*

crisp oats trail mix

1 cup gluten-free oats
½ cup unsalted shelled pumpkin seeds
½ cup dried sweetened cranberries
½ cup raisins
2 tablespoons maple syrup
1 teaspoon canola oil
½ teaspoon ground cinnamon
¼ teaspoon salt

1. Preheat oven to 325°F. Line baking sheet with heavy-duty foil.

2. Combine oats, pumpkin seeds, cranberries, raisins, maple syrup, oil, cinnamon and salt in large bowl. Stir well. Spread on prepared baking sheet. Bake 20 minutes or until oats are lightly browned, stirring halfway through. Serve as a snack or with dairy-free milk for breakfast. *Makes 2½ cups*

chocolate gingersnaps

¾ cup sugar
1 package (15 ounces) gluten-free chocolate or devil's food cake mix
1 tablespoon ground ginger
2 eggs
⅓ cup vegetable oil

1. Preheat oven to 350°F. Grease two cookie sheets or line with parchment paper. Place sugar in shallow bowl.

2. Combine cake mix and ginger in large bowl. Add eggs and oil; stir until well blended. Shape tablespoonfuls of dough into 1-inch balls; roll in sugar to coat. Place 2 inches apart on prepared cookie sheets.

3. Bake 10 minutes or until set. Cool on cookie sheets 2 minutes. Remove to wire racks; cool completely. *Makes about 3 dozen cookies*

old-fashioned chocolate chip cookies

6 tablespoons dairy-free soy-free margarine
6 tablespoons granulated sugar
6 tablespoons packed dark brown sugar
½ cup unsweetened applesauce
2 cups all-purpose flour
1 teaspoon baking soda
½ teaspoon baking powder
½ teaspoon salt
1 cup allergen-free chocolate chips
½ cup roasted unsalted sunflower seeds

1. Preheat oven to 350°F. Line baking sheet with parchment paper.

2. Beat margarine, granulated sugar and brown sugar in large bowl with electric mixer at medium speed until light. Beat in applesauce. Stir together flour, baking soda, baking powder and salt in medium bowl. Add to sugar mixture, ½ cup at a time, beating after each addition. Beat in chocolate chips and sunflower seeds.

3. Drop batter by heaping tablespoonfuls 1 inch apart on prepared baking sheet. Bake 16 to 18 minutes or until cookies are lightly browned. Cool on baking sheet 5 minutes. Remove to rack to cool completely. Store cookies in covered container or freeze.

Makes 3 dozen cookies

classic chili

1½ pounds ground beef
1½ cups chopped onion
1 cup chopped green bell pepper
2 cloves garlic, minced
3 cans (about 15 ounces each) dark red kidney beans, rinsed and drained
2 cans (about 15 ounces each) tomato sauce
1 can (about 14 ounces) diced tomatoes
2 to 3 teaspoons chili powder
1 teaspoon dry mustard
¾ teaspoon dried basil
½ teaspoon black pepper
    Shredded dairy-free cheese alternative

Slow Cooker Directions

1. Cook and stir beef, onion, bell pepper and garlic in large skillet over medium-high heat 6 to 8 minutes or until meat is browned and onion is tender. Drain fat. Transfer beef mixture to slow cooker.

2. Add beans, tomato sauce, tomatoes, chili powder, mustard, basil, black pepper and chile peppers, if desired; mix well. Cover; cook on LOW 8 to 10 hours or on HIGH 4 to 5 hours.

3. Sprinkle with cheese alternative before serving.   *Makes 6 servings*

> Most chili powders and dried mustards are free of common allergens. If you see "mustard flour" as the ingredient in dry mustard that just means mustard seeds were ground into flour, not that there is wheat flour added. A frequent problem with condiments is cross contamination. If someone used a spoon to stir or measure flour and then used it to measure chili powder, there may be residual gluten in the jar.

chocolate sandwich cookies

¾ cup dairy-free soy-free margarine, divided
1 package (15 ounces) gluten-free chocolate or devil's food cake mix
1 tablespoon tapioca flour
3 tablespoons unsweetened cocoa powder, divided
1 egg
4 to 5 tablespoons vanilla rice milk, divided
1½ cups powdered sugar
Creamy White Frosting (page 136)

1. Preheat oven to 350°F. Line baking sheet with parchment paper.

2. Melt ½ cup margarine in small saucepan over low heat. Combine cake mix, tapioca flour, 1 tablespoon cocoa, melted margarine, egg and 2 tablespoons rice milk in large bowl. Beat at medium speed 1 minute or until blended and batter comes together. Add 1 tablespoon rice milk, if needed.

3. Shape batter by level tablespoonfuls into balls; place 1 inch apart on baking sheet. Bake 10 minutes. Cookies will puff up but be very delicate. Cool on baking sheet 10 minutes. Remove to wire rack to cool completely.

4. For filling, beat remaining ¼ cup margarine, 2 tablespoons cocoa, 2 tablespoons rice milk and powdered sugar in large bowl with electric mixer at high speed until light and fluffy, scraping down bowl occasionally. Or prepare Creamy White Frosting to use as filling.

5. Spread scant tablespoon filling on half of cookies. Top with remaining cookies.

Makes 18 sandwich cookies

Lunch Hour

finger-lickin' chicken salad

 free from d e g n p

½ cup diced cooked chicken breast
½ stalk celery, cut into 1-inch pieces
¼ cup drained mandarin orange segments
¼ cup red seedless grapes
2 tablespoons dairy-free yogurt
1 tablespoon egg-free (vegan) mayonnaise
¼ teaspoon gluten-free soy sauce
⅛ teaspoon pumpkin pie spice or cinnamon

1. Toss chicken, celery, oranges and grapes together in small bowl.

2. Combine yogurt, mayonnaise, soy sauce and pumpkin pie spice in another small bowl or cup. Serve as dipping sauce with chicken mixture.

Makes 1 serving

soy-free variation: Replace yogurt dipping sauce with honey mustard or barbecue sauce.

variation: Thread the chicken onto wooden skewers alternately with celery, oranges and grapes.

note: This salad is a quick and nutritious meal for kids on the go. Pack the chicken mixture and dipping sauce in covered plastic containers, then pack them into an insulated bag with a frozen juice box.

eggless egg salad sandwiches

1 package (14 ounces) firm tofu, pressed* and crumbled
1 large stalk celery, finely diced
2 green onions, minced
2 tablespoons minced parsley
¼ cup plus 1 tablespoon egg-free (vegan) mayonnaise
3 tablespoons sweet pickle relish
2 teaspoons fresh lemon juice
1 teaspoon mustard
　Salt and black pepper
10 slices whole wheat bread
1½ cups alfalfa sprouts
10 tomato slices

To press tofu, cut in half horizontally and place between layers of paper towels. Place a weighted cutting board on top; let stand 15 to 30 minutes.

1. Combine tofu, celery, green onions and parsley in large bowl. Stir mayonnaise, relish, lemon juice, mustard, salt and pepper in small bowl until well blended. Add to tofu mixture; mix well.

2. Serve salad on bread topped with alfalfa sprouts and tomato slices.

Makes 5 sandwiches

gluten-free variation: Replace whole wheat bread with gluten-free Multi-Grain Sandwich Bread (page 72, NOT dairy-free) or serve with corn tortillas.

froggy bento box

dairy-free ranch dressing
   4 teaspoons soymilk or other dairy-free milk
   ¾ teaspoon lemon juice
   1 cup egg-free (vegan) mayonnaise
   1 tablespoon chopped fresh parsley
   1 tablespoon chopped fresh chives
   ½ teaspoon dried dill weed
   ¼ teaspoon onion powder
   ¼ teaspoon salt
   ⅛ teaspoon black pepper

lily pond
   ⅔ cup sushi rice or other short grain rice
   1 cup water
   ¼ teaspoon salt
      Blue paste food coloring
      Assorted sliced gluten-free lunch meat
   1 small seedless cucumber
      Carrot slices cut into fish shapes
      Assorted raw vegetables, such as lettuce, celery sticks, pea pods and grape
         tomatoes

1. For Ranch Dressing, combine soymilk and lemon juice in small bowl. Let stand 10 minutes. Meanwhile, whisk mayonnaise, parsley, chives, dill weed, onion powder, salt and pepper in medium bowl. Stir in soymilk mixture and refrigerate at least 30 minutes to blend flavors.

2. For Lily Pond, place rice in fine mesh strainer; rinse under cold water 1 minute. Combine rice, 1 cup water, salt and food coloring in small heavy saucepan; bring to a simmer. Reduce heat to low; cover and cook 15 minutes or until water is absorbed and rice is tender. Let stand, covered, 10 minutes.

3. Fill bottom of one section of bento box with blue rice. (Refrigerate extra rice for another use.) To make lily pads, cut small circles from lunch meat. Cut cucumber into small rounds. Make stacks of lunch meat and cucumber rounds. Position lily pads on blue rice. Place carrot fish between lily pads.

4. Line second section of bento box with lettuce and arrange raw vegetables and dressing in small container. (Refrigerate remaining dressing for another use.)

Makes 1 bento box

note: Bento boxes are Japanese-style lunch boxes. They can be purchased online.

vegetable chicken noodle soup

1 cup chopped celery
½ cup thinly sliced leek (white part only)
½ cup chopped carrots
½ cup chopped turnip
6 cups gluten-free soy-free chicken broth, divided
1 tablespoon minced fresh parsley
1½ teaspoons minced fresh thyme *or* ½ teaspoon dried thyme
1 teaspoon minced fresh rosemary leaves *or* ¼ teaspoon dried rosemary
1 teaspoon balsamic vinegar
¼ teaspoon black pepper
2 ounces uncooked gluten-free noodles
1 cup chopped cooked chicken

1. Combine celery, leek, carrots, turnip and ⅓ cup chicken broth in large saucepan. Cover; cook over medium heat 12 to 15 minutes or until vegetables are tender, stirring occasionally.

2. Stir in remaining 5⅔ cups broth, parsley, thyme, rosemary, vinegar and pepper; bring to a boil. Add noodles; cook until noodles are tender.

3. Stir in chicken. Reduce heat to medium; simmer until heated through.

Makes 6 servings

Fortunately, finding gluten-free pasta and noodles is easy these days. They're available made from quinoa, rice and corn flour among other blends. Different kinds require different cooking times so check the package directions. Gluten-free pasta tends to be softer than wheat pasta, so don't overcook it and add oil to the cooking water if the package suggests it.

tortilla pizza wedges

Nonstick cooking spray
1 cup frozen corn, thawed
1 cup thinly sliced fresh mushrooms
4 (6-inch) corn tortillas
¼ cup gluten-free soy-free pasta or pizza sauce
1 to 2 teaspoons chopped jalapeño pepper*
¼ teaspoon dried oregano
¼ teaspoon dried marjoram
½ cup (2 ounces) shredded part-skim mozzarella cheese

*Jalapeño peppers can sting and irritate the skin, so wear rubber gloves when handling peppers and do not touch your eyes.

1. Preheat oven to 450°F. Spray large skillet with cooking spray; heat over medium heat. Add corn and mushrooms; cook and stir 4 to 5 minutes or until tender.

2. Place tortillas on baking sheet. Bake 4 minutes or until edges begin to brown.

3. Combine pasta sauce, jalapeño, oregano and marjoram in small bowl. Spread over tortillas. Top evenly with corn and mushrooms. Sprinkle with cheese.

4. Bake 4 to 5 minutes or until cheese is melted and pizzas are heated through. Cut each pizza into four wedges.

Makes 4 servings

taco casserole

2 pounds ground beef
1 teaspoon salt
1 teaspoon garlic powder
1 teaspoon cumin
1 teaspoon paprika
1 teaspoon chili powder
½ teaspoon ground red pepper
1 can (10 ounces) diced tomatoes with green chiles
1 bag (12 ounces) corn tortilla chips, crushed
½ cup chopped green onions

1. Preheat oven to 375°F.

2. Brown beef in large skillet over medium-high heat 6 to 8 minutes, stirring to break up meat; drain fat. Stir in salt, garlic powder, cumin, paprika, chili powder and ground red pepper. Add tomatoes; cook and stir 3 minutes.

3. Stir in chips. Transfer to 13×9-inch casserole.

4. Bake 15 to 20 minutes or until heated through. Sprinkle with onions.

Makes 4 to 6 servings

beanie burgers

1 can (about 15 ounces) red kidney beans, rinsed and drained
½ cup chopped onion
⅓ cup gluten-free oats
1 egg
1 tablespoon gluten-free taco seasoning mix or mild chili powder
½ teaspoon salt
   Nonstick cooking spray
   Gluten-free hamburger buns, toasted (optional)
   Lettuce and tomato
   Salsa, mustard and other condiments

1. Combine beans, onion, oats, egg, taco seasoning and salt in food processor. Pulse until mixture is chunky. (Mixture may be made up to 1 day in advance. Cover and refrigerate until needed.)

2. Spray large skillet with cooking spray; heat over medium heat. Spoon bean mixture into 4 mounds in skillet, spreading into patties with back of spoon.

3. Cook 8 to 10 minutes. Serve on buns, if desired, with lettuce, tomato and condiments.   *Makes 4 servings*

Check ingredient lists carefully. Some taco seasoning mixes contain gluten, soy or dairy in the form of whey. To make your own allergen-free taco seasoning, combine 2 tablespoons of chili powder, 1 tablespoon of paprika, 2 teaspoons of onion powder, 1 teaspoon of cumin, ½ teaspoon of garlic powder, salt and pepper. Add a pinch of ground red pepper if you want a bit of heat.

chicken & sweet potato chili

1 to 2 sweet potatoes, peeled and cut into ½-inch chunks
2 teaspoons canola oil
1 cup chopped onion
¾ pound boneless skinless chicken breasts, cut into ¾-inch chunks
3 cloves garlic, minced
2 teaspoons chili powder
1 can (about 14 ounces) diced fire-roasted tomatoes
1 can (15 ounces) kidney beans or pinto beans, drained
½ cup chipotle or jalapeño salsa

1. Place sweet potatoes in large saucepan; add water to cover. Bring to a boil over high heat. Reduce heat; simmer 5 minutes or until almost tender. Drain sweet potatoes and set aside. Add oil and onion to same saucepan; cook and stir over medium heat 5 minutes.

2. Add chicken, garlic and chili powder; cook 3 minutes, stirring frequently. Add tomatoes, beans, salsa and partially cooked sweet potatoes; bring to a boil over high heat. Reduce heat; simmer uncovered 10 minutes or until chicken is cooked through and sweet potatoes are tender. *Makes 4 servings (1½ cups per serving)*

what a grape salad

1½ cups green and/or red seedless grapes, cut in half
1 red apple (such as Gala, Jonathan or Braeburn), cored and diced
½ cup finely diced celery
1 tablespoon golden raisins
½ cup egg-free (vegan) mayonnaise
2 tablespoons dairy-free yogurt
2 tablespoons crushed gluten-free cereal

Combine grapes, apple, celery and raisins in medium bowl. Mix mayonnaise and yogurt in small bowl. Gently stir into grape mixture. (Salad may be made up to 1 day ahead. Store in an airtight container and refrigerate until serving time.) Sprinkle each serving with cereal.   *Makes 4 (¾ cup) servings*

south-of-the-border lunch express

½ cup chopped seeded tomato
¼ cup chunky salsa
¼ cup rinsed and drained canned black beans
¼ cup frozen corn, thawed
1 teaspoon chopped fresh cilantro
¼ teaspoon chopped garlic
   Dash ground red pepper
1 cup cooked brown rice

Microwave Directions

1. Combine tomato, salsa, beans, corn, cilantro, garlic and red pepper in 1-quart microwavable bowl. Cover with vented plastic wrap. Microwave on HIGH 1 to 1½ minutes or until heated through; stir.

2. Microwave rice in separate 1-quart microwavable dish on HIGH 1 to 1½ minutes or until heated through. Top with tomato mixture.   *Makes 1 serving*

pumpkin seed spread

1 cup shelled raw pumpkin seeds
2½ tablespoons honey or agave syrup
½ teaspoon ground cinnamon
¼ teaspoon salt
2 to 4 tablespoons olive or vegetable oil

1. Preheat oven to 350°F. Spread pumpkin seeds on baking sheet. Bake 8 to 10 minutes or until seeds are golden. Cool to room temperature.

2. Place seeds in food processor; pulse until finely ground and powdery. Add honey, cinnamon and salt. Pulse to combine. Gradually add olive oil with machine running. Process 3 to 4 minutes or until smooth paste forms. Serve in place of peanut butter.

Makes about ¾ cup

herbivore dino wraps

1 seedless cucumber
12 lettuce leaves
6 ounces whipped cream cheese
¼ cup chopped fresh mint leaves
1¾ cups shredded carrots (about 3 medium carrots)
½ cup raisins

1. Trim cucumber; cut crosswise into 3-inch pieces. Cut into thin strips.

2. For each wrap, place 1 lettuce leaf on work surface. Spread with 1 tablespoon cream cheese in a lengthwise strip. Place 3 to 4 cucumber slices crosswise on cream cheese. Sprinkle with carrots, mint and raisins.

3. Fold sides of lettuce leaves over filling; roll up from bottom. Refrigerate until serving time.

Makes 12 wraps

chicken tortilla soup

2 tablespoons canola oil
½ cup finely chopped onion
½ cup finely chopped carrot
2½ cups shredded cooked chicken
1 cup thick and chunky salsa
4 cups gluten-free soy-free chicken broth
1 tablespoon lime juice
1 avocado, chopped
Corn tortilla chips

1. Heat oil in large saucepan over high heat. Add onion and carrot; cook and stir 3 minutes or until onion is translucent.

2. Stir in chicken and salsa. Add broth; bring to a boil. Reduce heat to medium-low; cover and simmer 5 minutes or until carrot is crisp-tender. Remove from heat; stir in lime juice.

3. Top with avocado and tortilla chips before serving.

Makes 5 (1½-cup) servings

Chicken soup is a lunchtime kids' classic. That old standby, canned chicken soup, is convenient, but can also have a long ingredient list with potential allergens. This homemade soup is quick and easy to put together and you control exactly what goes into it.

ham roll bento box

⅔ cup sushi rice
1 cup water
2 teaspoons sugar
⅛ teaspoon salt
2 tablespoons rice vinegar
2 slices deli ham (about 4 inches long)
1 roasted red bell pepper, cut into lengthwise strips
Honey or Dijon mustard
Cucumber Flowers (recipe follows)

1. Place rice in a fine mesh strainer. Rinse under cold running water for 1 minute. Place in small saucepan; stir in 1 cup water. Bring to a simmer; cover and cook 11 to 14 minutes or until water is absorbed and rice is tender. Remove from heat. Let stand, covered, 10 minutes.

2. Combine sugar, salt and rice vinegar in small saucepan. Bring to a simmer and stir to dissolve sugar. Pour over rice and mix gently. Set aside to cool.

3. Place 1 ham slice on work surface. Mound about 2 tablespoons rice along length of ham in center. Arrange pepper strip over rice. Tightly roll into 4-inch tube. Repeat with remaining ham slice, rice and pepper. Cut each ham roll into 1-inch pieces. Pack one compartment of bento with ham rolls and container of mustard for dipping. Pack another compartment with remaining rice topped with cucumber flowers. Include vegetables, fruit or dessert in other compartments.   *Makes 1 bento box*

cucumber flowers: Cut 6 thin slices from 1 small cucumber. Place ½ teaspoon prepared hummus in center of each slice. Top with half of grape tomato.

multi-grain sandwich bread

1 cup brown rice flour, plus additional for dusting pan
1 tablespoon active dry yeast
1¾ cups warm water (110°F)
2 tablespoons honey
¾ cup white rice flour
⅔ cup dry milk powder
½ cup gluten-free oat flour
⅓ cup cornstarch
⅓ cup potato starch
¼ cup teff flour
2 teaspoons xanthan gum
2 teaspoons egg white powder
1½ teaspoons sea salt
1 teaspoon unflavored gelatin
2 eggs
¼ cup canola oil

1. Preheat oven to 350°F. Grease 10×5-inch loaf pan. Dust with brown rice flour.

2. Sprinkle yeast over warm water in medium bowl. Add honey. Cover with plastic wrap; let stand 10 minutes or until foamy.

3. Combine brown rice flour, white rice flour, dry milk powder, oat flour, cornstarch, potato starch, teff flour, xanthan gum, egg white powder, salt and gelatin in large bowl. Mix until well blended.

4. Beat eggs in small bowl; whisk in oil.

5. Add yeast mixture and egg mixture to flour mixture. Beat with electric mixer at high speed 5 minutes. Transfer to prepared pan.

6. Bake 1 hour or until internal temperature is 200°F. Cool in pan on wire rack 5 minutes. Remove from pan to cool completely.

Makes 1 loaf

Family Dinner

oven-fried chicken

 free from

  6 boneless skinless chicken thighs
  ½ cup rice milk
  ½ cup corn flour (not cornmeal)
  2 tablespoons dairy-free soy-free margarine, melted
1½ cups crushed gluten-free cornflakes
  ½ teaspoon salt
  ¼ teaspoon garlic powder
  ½ teaspoon paprika
  ¼ teaspoon black pepper

1. Place chicken in medium bowl. Add rice milk; refrigerate 1 hour. Discard rice milk; pat chicken dry. Preheat oven to 350°F. Spray rimmed baking sheet with nonstick cooking spray.

2. Lightly dust chicken with corn flour. Brush with melted spread. Combine cornflakes, salt, garlic powder, paprika and pepper on a plate. Press chicken into mixture, generously coating both sides. Arrange on prepared baking sheet. Bake 35 to 40 minutes or until cooked through, turning chicken over after 20 minutes. *Makes 4 to 6 servings*

apple-stuffed acorn squash

free from

- ¼ cup raisins
- 2 acorn squash (about 4 inches in diameter)
- Olive oil cooking spray
- 2 tablespoons sugar
- ½ teaspoon ground cinnamon
- 2 medium Fuji apples
- 2 tablespoons dairy-free soy-free margarine

1. Place raisins in small bowl. Cover with warm water and soak 20 minutes. Preheat oven to 375°F.

2. Cut acorn squash into quarters; remove seeds. Place squash in baking dish. Spray inside of each squash quarter with cooking spray. Combine sugar and cinnamon in small bowl; sprinkle squash quarters with half of cinnamon mixture. Bake 10 minutes.

3. Meanwhile, chop apples into ½-inch pieces. Drain raisins. Melt margarine in saucepan over medium heat. Add apples, raisins and remaining cinnamon mixture; cook and stir 1 minute. Top partially baked squash with apple mixture. Bake 30 to 35 minutes or until apples and squash are tender. Serve warm.

Makes 8 servings

> This recipe makes a great side dish for a grilled main course or roast chicken or turkey. Use any winter squash—Delicata squash or butternut squash would also be delicious. Take care when cutting a hard squash. Use a sharp knife, a large cutting board and keep the squash stable. To make things easier, pierce the skin in a few places and microwave for 1 minute. Let the squash cool before cutting into it.

thai meatballs & noodles

Thai Meatballs (recipe follows)
12 ounces uncooked rice noodles
2 cans (about 14 ounces each) gluten-free chicken broth
2 tablespoons packed brown sugar
2 tablespoons gluten-free soy sauce
1 small piece fresh ginger, minced
1 medium carrot, cut into matchstick-size strips
1 pound bok choy, cut into ½-inch-wide strips
½ cup slivered fresh mint or basil leaves

1. Prepare Thai Meatballs. Place noodles in large bowl. Cover with hot water. Soak 15 to 20 minutes or until soft; drain and keep warm.

2. Heat broth in large saucepan or wok over high heat. Add brown sugar, soy sauce and ginger; stir until sugar is dissolved. Add meatballs and carrot; bring to a boil. Reduce heat to medium-low; cover and simmer 15 minutes or until meatballs are heated through. Add bok choy; simmer 4 to 5 minutes or until stalks are crisp-tender. Stir in mint; serve with noodles.

Makes 6 servings

thai meatballs

1½ pounds ground beef or pork
¼ cup chopped fresh basil leaves
¼ cup chopped fresh mint leaves
2 tablespoons finely chopped fresh ginger
1 tablespoon gluten-free soy sauce
6 cloves garlic, minced
1 teaspoon ground cinnamon
½ teaspoon black pepper
1 tablespoon vegetable oil

1. Combine beef, basil, mint, ginger, soy sauce, garlic, cinnamon and pepper in large bowl; mix until well blended. Shape into 1-inch balls.

2. Heat oil in large skillet or wok over medium-high heat. Add meatballs in batches; cook 8 to 10 minutes or until no longer pink in center, turning to brown all sides.

Makes about 32 meatballs

three-pepper steak

1 boneless beef top sirloin or beef flank steak (about 1 pound)
3 tablespoons gluten-free soy sauce
1 tablespoon cornstarch
1 tablespoon brown sugar
1½ teaspoons dark sesame oil
¼ teaspoon red pepper flakes
3 tablespoons olive oil, divided
1 small green bell pepper, cut into strips
1 small red bell pepper, cut into strips
1 small yellow bell pepper, cut into strips
1 medium onion, chopped
2 cloves garlic, minced
Hot cooked rice

1. Cut beef in half lengthwise, then crosswise into ¼-inch-thick slices. Combine soy sauce, cornstarch, brown sugar, sesame oil and red pepper flakes in medium bowl; stir until smooth. Add beef and toss to coat; set aside.

2. Heat wok over high heat 1 minute. Drizzle 1 tablespoon oil into wok and heat 30 seconds. Add bell pepper strips; stir-fry until crisp-tender. Remove to large bowl. Heat 1 tablespoon vegetable oil in wok 30 seconds. Add half of beef mixture; stir-fry until well browned. Remove beef to bowl with bell peppers. Repeat with remaining 1 tablespoon vegetable oil and half of beef mixture.

3. Reduce heat to medium. Add onion; stir-fry 3 minutes or until softened. Add garlic; stir-fry 30 seconds. Return bell peppers, beef and any accumulated juices to wok; cook until heated through. Serve beef and vegetables over rice.   *Makes 4 servings*

spanish chicken with rice

free from

2 tablespoons olive oil
1 package (about 14 ounces) gluten-free cooked smoked sausage, sliced
    into ½-inch rounds
6 boneless skinless chicken thighs
1 onion, chopped
5 cloves garlic, minced
2 cups converted long grain white rice
½ cup diced carrots
1 red bell pepper, chopped
½ teaspoon salt
¼ teaspoon black pepper
¼ teaspoon saffron threads, crushed (optional)
3½ cups hot gluten-free soy-free chicken broth
½ cup peas

Slow Cooker Directions

1. Heat oil in medium skillet over medium heat. Add sausage and brown on both sides. Transfer to slow cooker with slotted spoon.

2. Add chicken to skillet and brown on all sides. Transfer to slow cooker. Add onion to skillet; cook and stir 2 to 3 minutes or until translucent. Stir in garlic and cook 30 seconds. Transfer to slow cooker.

3. Add rice, carrots, bell pepper, salt, black pepper and saffron, if desired, to slow cooker. Pour broth over mixture. Cover; cook on HIGH 3½ to 4 hours or until chicken is cooked through. Stir in peas 15 minutes before end of cooking time.

Makes 6 servings

vegetarian paella

2 teaspoons canola oil
1 cup chopped onion
2 cloves garlic, minced
1 cup uncooked brown rice
2¼ cups gluten-free soy-free vegetable broth
1 teaspoon Italian seasoning
¾ teaspoon salt
½ teaspoon ground turmeric
⅛ teaspoon ground red pepper
1 can (14½ ounces) stewed tomatoes
1 cup chopped red bell pepper
1 cup coarsely chopped carrots
1 can (14 ounces) quartered artichoke hearts, drained
1 zucchini, sliced
½ cup frozen peas

1. Heat oil in large nonstick skillet over medium-high heat. Add onion and garlic; cook 6 to 7 minutes or until onion is translucent. Reduce heat to medium-low. Stir in rice; cook and stir 1 minute.

2. Add broth, Italian seasoning, salt, turmeric and ground red pepper. Bring to a boil. Cover and simmer 30 minutes.

3. Stir in tomatoes, bell pepper and carrots. Cover and simmer 10 minutes.

4. Reduce heat to low. Stir in artichoke hearts, zucchini and peas. Cover and cook 10 minutes or until rice and vegetables are tender. ***Makes 6 servings***

mom's spaghetti sauce

7½ cups water
3 cans (15 ounces each) tomato puree
3 cans (6 ounces each) tomato paste*
1 can (about 14 ounces) diced tomatoes
2 large onions, chopped
3 tablespoons sugar
2 tablespoons salt
1½ tablespoons Italian seasoning
1½ tablespoons dried oregano
1 tablespoon black pepper
6 cloves garlic, minced
3 bay leaves
3 pounds ground beef, shaped into about 35 meatballs and browned
2 to 2½ pounds gluten-free Italian sausage (optional)
    Gluten-free spaghetti or other pasta

Add more tomato paste if thicker sauce is desired.

Slow Cooker Directions

1. Combine all ingredients except sausage and meatballs in large bowl; mix well. Divide mixture between two slow cookers. Cover; cook on HIGH 1 hour.

2. Divide meatballs and sausage, if desired, between slow cookers. Cover; cook on LOW 6 to 8 hours. Serve over hot gluten-free spaghetti or any other type of gluten-free pasta. Freeze half of sauce for another use.   *Makes 10 servings*

chicken pot pie

2 tablespoons dairy-free soy-free margarine
1 small onion, chopped
3 tablespoons all-purpose flour
2 cups soy-free chicken broth
¼ teaspoon dried thyme
¼ teaspoon salt
¼ teaspoon black pepper
2 cups chopped cooked chicken
1 cup frozen green beans, cut into bite-size pieces
1 cup frozen corn
Drop Biscuits (recipe follows)

1. Preheat oven to 350°F. Melt margarine in large skillet or Dutch oven. Add onion; cook and stir over medium heat 5 minutes. Stir in flour. Gradually add broth, stirring constantly, until mixture thickens. Stir in thyme, salt and pepper. Add chicken, green beans and corn. Cook over medium heat 5 minutes or until vegetables thaw.

2. Spoon chicken mixture into shallow 10-inch casserole. Prepare Drop Biscuits. Spoon biscuit batter onto casserole to make 8 small biscuits. Bake 30 minutes or until biscuits are cooked through.   *Makes 4 servings*

drop biscuits

1 cup all-purpose flour
2 teaspoons baking powder
1 teaspoon sugar
¼ teaspoon salt
4 tablespoons dairy-free soy-free margarine
4 tablespoons rice milk

Stir together flour, baking powder, sugar and salt in medium bowl. Cut in margarine with pastry blender or two knives until mixture is crumbly. Add rice milk by tablespoonfuls to form wet, sticky dough.   *Makes 8 biscuits*

chili-topped potato boats

1 tablespoon canola oil
1 clove garlic, minced
1 small onion, chopped
1 small green bell pepper, chopped
1 pound ground beef
1 can (about 15 ounces) pinto or kidney beans, rinsed and drained
1 tablespoon tomato paste
1 cup crushed tomatoes
½ teaspoon ground cumin
1 teaspoon chili powder
¼ teaspoon chipotle chile powder
¾ teaspoon salt
¼ teaspoon black pepper
3 large baking potatoes, baked, halved lengthwise and scooped out

1. Heat oil in large nonstick skillet over medium heat. Add garlic, onion and bell pepper. Cook and stir 5 to 6 minutes or until onion is tender. Add beef; brown 6 to 8 minutes, stirring to break up meat. Drain fat. Stir in beans, tomato paste, tomatoes, cumin, chili powder, chipotle chile powder, salt and pepper.

2. Simmer 10 to 15 minutes or until heated through and flavors are blended. Spoon about ⅔ cup mixture into each potato half. *Makes 6 servings*

> Remember to check labels for allergens every time you purchase a prepared product, not just the first time. Formulations can change even if the brand and product are the same.

beef & bean enchiladas

free from

½ pound ground beef
1 can (about 15 ounces) pinto beans, drained and coarsely mashed
½ teaspoon ground cumin
½ teaspoon salt, divided
¼ teaspoon pepper, divided
1 tablespoon canola or other vegetable oil
1 small onion, chopped
1 small clove garlic, minced
1 small green bell pepper, chopped
1 small jalapeño pepper, seeded and minced (optional)
1 can (about 14 ounces) crushed tomatoes
1½ to 2 teaspoons chili powder
8 fresh corn tortillas, about 5 inches in diameter, softened according to package directions
1 small ripe avocado, cut into wedges (optional)

1. Preheat oven to 350°F. Brown beef in large nonstick skillet over medium heat, stirring to break up meat. Stir in beans, cumin, ¼ teaspoon salt and ⅛ teaspoon pepper. Remove from skillet; set aside.

2. For tomato sauce, heat oil in large skillet over medium heat. Add onion, garlic, bell pepper and jalapeño. Cook and stir 8 to 10 minutes or until onion is translucent. Stir in crushed tomatoes, remaining ¼ teaspoon salt, remaining ⅛ teaspoon pepper and chili powder. Reduce heat to low and simmer 5 minutes.

3. To assemble enchiladas, spoon ¼ cup bean mixture down center of each tortilla. Fold edges to center. Place in 9-inch square baking dish. Cover enchiladas with tomato sauce. Bake 20 minutes. Top enchiladas with avocado. *Makes 4 servings*

broccoli-tofu stir-fry

- 2 cups uncooked rice
- 1 can (14½ ounces) gluten-free vegetable broth, divided
- 3 tablespoons cornstarch
- 1 tablespoon gluten-free soy sauce
- ½ teaspoon sugar
- ¼ teaspoon dark sesame oil
- 1 package (about 16 ounces) extra-firm tofu, pressed*
- 1 teaspoon vegetable oil
- 1 tablespoon minced fresh ginger
- 3 cloves garlic, minced
- 3 cups broccoli florets
- 2 cups sliced mushrooms
- ½ cup chopped green onions
- 1 large red bell pepper, cut into strips

*To press tofu, cut it in half horizontally and place it between layers of paper towels. Place a weighted cutting board on top for 15 to 30 minutes.

1. Cook rice according to package directions. Combine ¼ cup vegetable broth, cornstarch, soy sauce, sugar and sesame oil in small bowl; set aside. Cut tofu into 1-inch cubes; set aside.

2. Heat oil in large nonstick skillet or wok over medium heat. Add ginger and garlic. Cook and stir 5 minutes. Add remaining vegetable broth, broccoli, mushrooms, green onions and bell pepper. Cook and stir over medium-high heat 5 minutes or until vegetables are crisp-tender. Add tofu; cook 2 minutes, stirring occasionally. Stir cornstarch mixture; add to vegetable mixture. Cook and stir until sauce thickens. Serve with rice.

Makes 6 servings

farm-style casserole

1 tablespoon canola oil
1 small onion, chopped
1 clove garlic, minced
1 pound ground beef
1 can (14½ ounces) diced tomatoes
1 cup frozen corn
1 cup frozen baby lima beans
1 teaspoon salt
½ teaspoon dried oregano
¼ teaspoon black pepper
2 cups cooked gluten-free macaroni or other pasta
1 cup crushed corn tortilla chips

1. Preheat oven to 350°F. Heat oil in large nonstick skillet over medium heat. Add onion and garlic; cook and stir 5 to 6 minutes or until onion is tender. Add beef; brown 6 to 8 minutes, stirring to break up meat. Drain fat.

2. Stir in tomatoes, corn, lima beans, salt, oregano and pepper. Increase heat to high; cook and stir 5 minutes or until excess liquid evaporates. Stir in pasta. Spoon mixture into 9-inch square baking dish. Sprinkle with tortilla chips. Bake 20 minutes or until heated through.

Makes 4 to 6 servings

> Customize this casserole to suit your family's taste preferences. You could substitute green beans or broccoli florets for the lima beans. Instead of tortilla chips, you could use crushed potato chips or coarse gluten-free bread crumbs. Adjust spices to your taste, too. Italian seasoning or chili powder would be delicious.

Family Dinner

Snack Safely

creamy strawberry-orange pops

 free from d e g n p

    8 ounces strawberry dairy-free yogurt
    ¾ cup orange juice
    2 teaspoons vanilla
    2 cups frozen whole strawberries
    2 teaspoons sugar
    6 (7-ounce) paper cups
    6 wooden sticks

1. Combine yogurt, orange juice and vanilla in food processor or blender. Cover and process until smooth.

2. Add strawberries and sugar. Process until smooth. Pour into paper cups, filling each about three-fourths full. Place in freezer for 1 hour. Insert wooden stick into center of each. Freeze completely. Peel cup off each pop to serve.

Makes 6 servings

gf graham crackers

 free from

½ cup sweet rice flour (mochiko), plus additional for rolling
½ cup sorghum flour
½ cup lightly packed brown sugar
⅓ cup tapioca flour
½ teaspoon baking soda
½ teaspoon salt
¼ cup dairy-free soy-free margarine
2 tablespoons plus 2 teaspoons rice milk
2 tablespoons honey
1 tablespoon vanilla

1. Combine sweet rice flour, sorghum flour, brown sugar, tapioca flour, baking soda and salt in bowl of food processor. Pulse to combine, making sure brown sugar is free of lumps. Add margarine and pulse until coarse crumbs form.

2. Stir together rice milk, honey and vanilla in measuring cup until honey dissolves. Pour into flour mixture and process until dough comes together. Dough will be very soft and sticky. Transfer dough to rice-floured surface; pat into rectangle. Wrap and refrigerate dough at least 4 hours or up to 2 days.

3. Preheat oven to 325°F. Cover work surface with parchment paper and generously flour parchment paper with rice flour.

4. Roll dough to ⅛-inch thick rectangle on parchment using floured rolling pin. If dough becomes too sticky, return to refrigerator or freezer for several minutes. Transfer dough on parchment paper to baking sheet. Score dough into cracker shapes (do not cut all the way through.) Prick dough in rows with tines of fork. Place baking sheet in freezer for 5 to 10 minutes or in refrigerator for 15 to 20 minutes.

5. Transfer cold crackers directly to oven; bake 25 minutes or until firm and a shade darker. Slide parchment onto wire rack to cool. Cut crackers apart when cooled slightly.

Makes about 1 dozen crackers

s'mores: Place allergen-free chocolate squares on GF Graham Crackers. Top with toasted marshmallows and additional GF Graham Crackers.

applesauce-spice bread

1½ cups Gluten-Free All-Purpose Flour Blend (page 16)
1½ cups unsweetened applesauce
¾ cup packed light brown sugar
½ cup shortening
1 teaspoon vanilla
1 teaspoon baking soda
1 teaspoon ground cinnamon
¾ teaspoon xanthan gum
½ teaspoon baking powder
¼ teaspoon salt
¼ teaspoon ground nutmeg
½ cup toasted chopped walnuts
½ cup raisins
Powdered sugar

1. Preheat oven to 350°F. Spray 9-inch square baking pan with nonstick cooking spray.

2. Beat flour blend, applesauce, brown sugar, shortening, vanilla, baking soda, cinnamon, xanthan gum, baking powder, salt and nutmeg in large bowl with electric mixer at low speed 30 seconds. Increase speed to high; beat 3 minutes. Stir in walnuts and raisins. Pour into prepared pan.

3. Bake 30 minutes or until toothpick inserted into center comes out clean. Cool in pan on wire rack. Sprinkle with powdered sugar before serving. *Makes 9 servings*

taco boulders

2¼ cups gluten-free biscuit baking mix
1 cup (4 ounces) shredded taco cheese
2 tablespoons diced mild green chiles
⅔ cup milk
3 tablespoons butter, melted
¼ teaspoon chili powder
¼ teaspoon garlic powder

1. Preheat oven to 425°F. Line baking sheet with parchment paper or spray with nonstick cooking spray.

2. Combine baking mix, cheese and chiles in large bowl. Stir in milk just until moistened. Drop dough by ¼ cupfuls into 12 mounds on prepared baking sheet.

3. Bake 11 to 13 minutes or until golden brown. Meanwhile, combine melted butter, chili powder and garlic powder in small bowl. Remove biscuits to wire rack; immediately brush with butter mixture. Serve warm. *Makes 12 biscuits*

monkey parfaits

1 banana, sliced
8 ounces strawberry dairy-free yogurt
1 cup seedless red grapes or pitted cherries, halved
½ cup flaked coconut
½ cup mandarin oranges, drained
4 grapes or pitted cherries

Layer half of banana slices, yogurt, grapes, coconut and oranges four parfait glasses. Repeat layers. Top each serving with one whole grape. *Makes 4 servings*

happy apple salsa with baked cinnamon pita chips

2 teaspoons sugar
¼ teaspoon ground cinnamon
2 rounds pita bread, split
  Nonstick cooking spray
1 tablespoon jelly or jam
1 medium apple, diced
1 tablespoon finely diced celery
1 tablespoon finely diced carrot
1 tablespoon golden raisins
1 teaspoon lemon juice

1. Preheat oven to 350°F.

2. Combine sugar and cinnamon in small bowl. Cut pitas into wedges; place on ungreased baking sheet. Spray lightly with cooking spray; sprinkle with cinnamon-sugar. Bake 10 minutes or until lightly browned. Set aside to cool.

3. Meanwhile, place jelly in medium microwavable bowl; microwave on HIGH 10 seconds. Stir in apple, celery, carrot, raisins and lemon juice. Serve salsa with pita chips.

Makes 2 servings

> If your child is sensitive to gluten, serve this salsa with rice crackers or other gluten-free crackers. Add a bit of cinnamon-sugar to the salsa.

chocolate chip elvis bread

2½ cups Gluten-Free All-Purpose Flour Blend (page 16)
½ cup granulated sugar
½ cup packed brown sugar
1 tablespoon baking powder
¾ teaspoon salt
1 teaspoon xanthan gum
1 cup mashed ripe bananas (about 2 large)
1 cup rice milk
¾ cup peanut butter
¼ cup vegetable oil
Prepared powdered egg replacer equal to 1 egg
1 teaspoon vanilla
1 cup allergen-free chocolate chips

1. Preheat oven to 350°F. Spray four mini (5½×3-inch) loaf pans with nonstick cooking spray.

2. Combine flour blend, granulated sugar, brown sugar, baking powder and salt in large bowl; mix well. Beat bananas, rice milk, peanut butter, oil, egg replacer and vanilla in medium bowl until well blended. Add banana mixture and chocolate chips to flour mixture; stir just until moistened. Pour into prepared pans.

3. Bake 40 minutes or until toothpick inserted into centers comes out clean. Cool in pans on wire racks 10 minutes. Remove from pans; cool completely on wire racks.

Makes 4 mini loaves

frosty orange bowls

2 small navel oranges
1 container (6 ounces) orange, lemon or vanilla dairy-free yogurt

1. Cut off top quarter of orange and discard. Cut small slice of rind off bottom to help orange stand upright. Remove pulp from each orange with small knife or grapefruit spoon.

2. Place orange pulp and yogurt in blender; blend 12 seconds or until almost smooth. Spoon mixture into orange shells, slightly mounding tops. (Pour any leftover mixture in small cup.)

3. Place filled oranges in small container or individual custard cups. Cover loosely with plastic wrap. Freeze 1 hour or until slightly firm. Oranges can be frozen up to several days. Let stand 15 to 30 minutes to soften.   *Makes 2 servings*

carrot stix

1 package (16 ounces) carrots
2 teaspoons olive oil
½ teaspoon salt
¼ teaspoon black pepper
1 teaspoon sugar
¼ teaspoon ground cinnamon

1. Preheat oven to 375°F. Line large baking sheet with foil.

2. Cut carrots in half crosswise. Cut each piece lengthwise into strips. Combine carrot sticks, oil, salt and pepper in large bowl. Toss to coat. Arrange carrots on prepared baking sheet. Bake 20 minutes, turning once.

3. Meanwhile, combine sugar and cinnamon in small bowl. Transfer baked carrots to large bowl. Sprinkle with sugar mixture; toss to coat. Serve immediately.

Makes 4 to 6 servings

note: One bag (16 ounces) of baby carrots can be substituted for the large carrots. Bake for 25 minutes.

snacking surprise muffins

 **free from** d g n p s

⅔ cup rice milk
2 teaspoons cider vinegar
1½ cups Gluten-Free All-Purpose Flour Blend (page 16)
1 cup fresh or frozen blueberries
½ cup plus 1 tablespoon sugar, divided
1 tablespoon baking powder
1¼ teaspoons ground cinnamon, divided
½ teaspoon xanthan gum
¼ teaspoon salt
1 egg, beaten
¼ cup dairy-free soy-free margarine, melted
3 tablespoons peach or apricot preserves

1. Preheat oven to 400°F. Line 12 standard (2½-inch) muffin cups with paper baking cups.

2. Combine rice milk and vinegar; let stand 10 minutes. Meanwhile, combine flour blend, blueberries, ½ cup sugar, baking powder, 1 teaspoon cinnamon, xanthan gum and salt in medium bowl. Add rice milk mixture, egg and margarine to flour mixture; mix just until moistened.

3. Spoon about 1 tablespoon batter into each muffin cup. Drop a scant teaspoonful of preserves into center of batter in each cup; top with remaining batter.

4. Combine remaining 1 tablespoon sugar and ¼ teaspoon cinnamon in small bowl; sprinkle evenly over batter.

5. Bake 18 to 20 minutes or until lightly browned. Cool in pan on wire rack 5 minutes. Remove from pan.

Makes 12 servings

zucchini bread

 free from g n p s

2½ cups All-Purpose Gluten-Free Flour Blend (page 16)
⅔ cup packed brown sugar
½ cup teff flour
⅓ cup granulated sugar
1 tablespoon baking powder
2 teaspoons ground cinnamon
1 teaspoon baking soda
1 teaspoon sea salt
¾ teaspoon xanthan gum
¼ teaspoon ground allspice
¼ teaspoon ground nutmeg
¼ teaspoon ground cardamom
1¼ cups milk
2 eggs
¼ cup canola oil
1 teaspoon vanilla
1½ cups grated zucchini, squeezed dry

1. Preheat oven to 350°F. Grease 9×5-inch loaf pan.

2. Combine flour blend, brown sugar, teff flour, granulated sugar, baking powder, cinnamon, baking soda, salt, xanthan gum, allspice, nutmeg and cardamom in large bowl. Mix well.

3. Whisk milk, eggs, oil and vanilla in medium bowl. Make well in center of dry ingredients. Stir in milk mixture. Gently stir in zucchini. Transfer to prepared pan.

4. Bake 1 hour or until toothpick inserted into center comes out almost clean. Cool in pan 5 minutes. Remove from pan to cool. *Makes 12 servings (1 loaf)*

colorful kabobs

30 cocktail-size gluten-free soy-free cooked smoked sausages
10 to 20 cherry or grape tomatoes
10 to 20 large pimiento-stuffed green olives
 2 yellow bell peppers, cut into 1-inch squares
¼ cup olive oil
   Lemon juice (optional)

1. Preheat oven to 450°F.

2. Thread sausages, tomatoes, olives and bell peppers alternately onto ten 8-inch skewers.

3. Place skewers on rack in shallow baking pan. Brush with oil and drizzle with lemon juice, if desired. Bake 4 to 6 minutes until hot.   *Makes 10 kabobs*

tip: For younger children, remove food from skewers and serve in a paper cup or bowl. It's still portable, but much safer.

banana caterpillars

2 medium bananas
¼ cup sunflower seed butter
¼ cup flaked coconut
4 raisins
6 thin gluten-free pretzel sticks

1. Peel bananas and cut crosswise into 10 slices. Assemble caterpillar by spreading slices with sunflower seed butter and pressing pieces together.

2. Sprinkle half of coconut over each caterpillar; press lightly to coat. Use additional sunflower seed butter to attach raisins for eyes.

3. Break pretzel sticks into small pieces; press between banana slices to create legs and antennae. *Makes 2 servings*

Tip: Kids can also be creative and add other types of sliced fruits (strawberries, apples, pears) to their caterpillars.

great green veggie wedgies

2 (8- to 10-inch) spinach tortillas
½ cup dairy-free cream cheese alternative
¼ cup apricot or peach fruit spread
½ cup coarsely chopped fresh baby spinach
¼ cup grated carrot

1. Evenly spread cream cheese over one side of each tortilla.

2. Spread fruit spread over cream cheese on one tortilla. Sprinkle spinach and carrots over fruit spread.

3. Top with second tortilla, cheese side down. Lightly press tortillas together. Cut into wedges. *Makes 2 servings*

Snack Safely

date & walnut bread

¾ cup chopped, pitted dates (8 to 10 Medjool dates)
1 cup boiling water
½ cup brown rice flour
½ cup almond flour
½ cup cornstarch
¼ cup tapioca flour
¼ cup gluten-free oat flour
1 tablespoon baking powder
1 teaspoon xanthan gum
1 teaspoon baking soda
½ teaspoon salt
½ teaspoon cardamom
1 cup packed brown sugar
¼ cup canola oil
2 eggs
1 teaspoon vanilla
1 cup walnuts, coarsely chopped

1. Preheat oven to 350°F. Grease 9×5-inch loaf pan. Pour boiling water over dates in small bowl; set aside until softened and cooled.

2. Whisk together brown rice flour, almond flour, cornstarch, tapioca flour, oat flour, baking powder, xanthan gum, baking soda, salt and cardamom in medium bowl.

3. Stir together brown sugar and oil in large bowl. Add eggs, one at a time, beating well after each addition. Stir in vanilla. Stir in dates and water.

4. Add flour mixture; stir just until combined. Stir in walnuts.

5. Pour into prepared pan. Bake 50 to 55 minutes or until toothpick inserted into center comes out clean. (Check after 35 minutes and cover with foil to prevent overbrowning, if necessary). Cool in pan on wire rack 10 minutes. Remove from pan to cool. *Makes 12 servings (1 loaf)*

Sweet Stuff

maple-oatmeal cookies

- ½ cup dairy-free soy-free margarine
- ½ cup packed light brown sugar
- ½ cup maple syrup
- 1½ cups old-fashioned oats
- ¾ cup all-purpose flour
- ½ teaspoon baking soda
- ½ teaspoon ground cinnamon
- ¼ teaspoon salt
- ½ cup raisins

1. Preheat oven to 375° F. Line baking sheet with parchment paper.

2. Place margarine, brown sugar and maple syrup in large bowl. Beat with electric mixer at medium speed 1 minute or until creamy. Mix oats, flour, baking soda, cinnamon and salt in medium bowl. Gradually add to sugar mixture, beating after each addition. Beat in raisins.

3. Drop batter by heaping tablespoonfuls 1 inch apart on prepared baking sheet. Flatten to ½ inch thick. Bake 13 to 16 minutes or until golden. Cool on baking sheet 5 minutes. Remove to wire rack. Serve warm.

Makes about 2 dozen cookies

allergy-free strawberry cake

1 package (15 ounces) gluten-free yellow cake mix
½ cup rice milk
½ cup dairy-free margarine
    Prepared powdered egg replacer equal to 3 eggs
2 teaspoons grated lemon peel
1 teaspoon vanilla
1 cup sliced strawberries
1 to 2 tablespoons powdered sugar
4 large strawberries, cut in half (optional)

1. Preheat oven to 350°F. Spray 9-inch round cake pan with nonstick cooking spray.

2. Beat cake mix, rice milk, margarine, egg replacer, lemon peel and vanilla in bowl of electric mixer. Beat at low speed 30 seconds. Increase speed to medium and beat 1 minute. Add sliced strawberries. Beat at medium speed 1 to 2 minutes or until strawberries are crushed. Spoon batter into prepared pan.

3. Bake 35 to 40 minutes or until cake is golden brown and firm to the touch. Cool in pan 10 minutes. Remove to wire rack; cool completely. Dust with powdered sugar. Garnish with strawberry halves.

Makes 8 servings

> Dealing with an egg allergy can be tricky when baking. Eggs serve many different functions in various recipes, from providing lightness to holding ingredients together. Powdered egg replacer works well for recipes like this one. Be aware that products labeled "egg substitute" are generally made from egg whites and cannot be used. They were created to allow people to enjoy eggs without cholesterol.

coconut milk ice cream

2 cans (13½ ounces each) unsweetened coconut milk
½ cup sugar
1 gluten-free dairy-free candy bar, crushed into small pieces (optional)

1. Combine coconut milk and sugar in medium saucepan. Cook over medium-low heat whisking constantly until smooth and sugar is dissolved. Refrigerate until cold.

2. Process in ice cream maker according to manufacturer's directions, adding candy pieces as directed. Transfer to freezer storage container and freeze until firm.

3. Let soften at room temperature or microwave for 30 to 40 seconds before serving to make scooping easy. *Makes about 1 quart*

> The FDA classifies coconut as a tree nut for the purposes of identifying common allergens. It seems, however, that many of those allergic to tree nuts, like almonds or walnuts, can tolerate coconut. It's worth discussing with your allergy specialist since many coconut products are available and they often work well to mimic the richness of dairy.

lots o' chocolate bread

2 cups mini allergen-free chocolate chips, divided
⅔ cup packed light brown sugar
½ cup dairy-free soy-free margarine
   Prepared powdered egg replacer equal to 2 eggs
2½ cups Gluten-Free All-Purpose Flour Blend (page 00)
1½ cups applesauce
1½ teaspoons vanilla
1½ teaspoons baking soda
1¼ teaspoons xanthan gum
1 teaspoon baking powder
½ teaspoon salt
1 tablespoon shortening (do not use margarine, spread or oil)

1. Preheat oven to 350°F. Grease 5 mini (5½×3-inch) loaf pans. Place 1 cup chocolate chips in small microwavable bowl. Microwave on HIGH 1 minute; stir. Microwave at 30-second intervals, stirring after each interval, until chocolate is melted and smooth.

2. Beat brown sugar and margarine in large bowl with electric mixer at medium speed until creamy. Add melted chocolate and egg replacer; beat until well blended. Add flour blend, applesauce, vanilla, baking soda, xanthan gum, baking powder and salt; beat until well blended. Stir in ½ cup chocolate chips. Spoon batter evenly into prepared pans.

3. Bake 35 to 40 minutes or until centers crack and are dry to the touch. Cool in pans on wire racks 10 minutes. Remove from pans; cool completely.

4. Place remaining ½ cup chocolate chips and shortening in small microwavable bowl. Microwave on HIGH 1 minute; stir. Microwave at 30-second intervals, stirring after each interval, until chocolate is melted and mixture is smooth. Drizzle loaves with glaze; let stand until set. *Makes 5 mini loaves*

very orange cake

1 package (15 ounces) gluten-free yellow cake mix
⅔ cup orange juice
½ cup (1 stick) dairy-free margarine
3 eggs
1 teaspoon vanilla
1 package (4-serving size) orange gelatin
½ cup boiling water
¼ cup cold water
Marshmallow Frosting (recipe follows)
Candy orange slices (optional)

1. Preheat oven to 350°F. Spray 9-inch square cake pan with nonstick cooking spray.

2. Beat cake mix, orange juice, margarine, eggs and vanilla in large bowl with electric mixer at low speed 30 seconds to combine. Beat at medium speed 2 minutes or until smooth. Pour batter into prepared pan.

3. Bake 40 to 50 minutes or until toothpick inserted into center comes out almost clean. Cool on wire rack.

4. Place half of orange gelatin powder in small bowl or measuring cup. (Discard remaining powder.) Stir ½ cup boiling water into gelatin until it dissolves completely. Stir in ¼ cup cold water. Poke cake at ½-inch intervals with fork or skewer. Pour gelatin mixture over cake. Refrigerate 2 to 3 hours or until firm.

5. Meanwhile, prepare Marshmallow Frosting. Frost cake and decorate with candy orange slices. *Makes 12 to 16 servings*

marshmallow frosting

1 jar (about 7 ounces) marshmallow creme
1 container (8 ounces) dairy-free cream cheese alternative
1 teaspoon vanilla

Beat marshmallow creme, cream cheese alternative and vanilla in large bowl until well blended and fluffy. *Makes about 2 cups frosting*

sunflower seed butter cookies

1 cup creamy sunflower seed butter*
1 cup sugar
1 egg
1 teaspoon vanilla
½ cup mini allergen-free chocolate chips

Do not use sunflower seed butter labeled "natural."

1. Preheat oven to 350°F. Line cookie sheet with parchment paper.

2. Combine sunflower seed butter, sugar, egg and vanilla in medium bowl. Stir until smooth and combined. Fold in chocolate chips. Drop dough by tablespoonfuls onto prepared cookie sheet. Flatten cookies in crisscross pattern with fork.

3. Bake 10 to 12 minutes or until firm. Do not overbake. Cool on cookie sheet 2 minutes; transfer to wire rack to cool completely.   *Makes 1 dozen cookies*

pink peppermint meringues

3 egg whites
⅛ teaspoon peppermint extract
5 drops red food coloring
½ cup superfine sugar
6 peppermint candies, finely crushed

1. Preheat oven to 200°F. Line cookie sheets with parchment paper.

2. Beat egg whites in medium bowl with electric mixer at medium-high speed 45 seconds or until frothy. Beat in peppermint extract and food coloring. Add sugar, 1 tablespoon at a time, while mixer is running. Beat until egg whites are stiff and glossy.

3. Drop meringue by teaspoonfuls into 1-inch mounds on prepared cookie sheets; sprinkle evenly with crushed candies.

4. Bake 2 hours or until meringues are dry when tapped. Transfer parchment paper with meringues to wire racks.   *Makes about 6 dozen meringues*

sweet cherry biscuits

free from

2 cups gluten-free biscuit baking mix
¼ cup sugar
2 teaspoons baking powder
½ teaspoon salt
½ teaspoon crushed dried rosemary
½ cup (1 stick) unsalted butter, cut into small pieces
¾ cup milk
½ cup dried cherries, chopped

1. Preheat oven to 425°F. Combine baking mix, sugar, baking powder, salt and rosemary in large bowl. Cut in butter with pastry blender or two knives until mixture forms small crumbs. Stir in milk to form sticky batter. Stir in cherries.

2. Pat dough to 1-inch thickness on surface lightly dusted with baking mix. Cut out circles with 3-inch biscuit cutter. Place biscuits 1 inch apart on ungreased baking sheet. Bake about 15 minutes or until golden brown. Cool on wire rack 5 minutes before serving.

Makes about 10 biscuits

> Gluten-free biscuit baking mix is sold under a few different brand names. They each contain a blend of GF flours as well as leavening and xanthan or guar gum. Some contain bean flours, sugar, almond meal and other ingredients you may wish to avoid. Read the labels and find one that fits your needs and pleases your taste buds.

fudgy chocolate pudding cake

free from d e n p s

- 1 cup granulated sugar, divided
- 1 cup all-purpose flour
- ½ cup unsweetened cocoa powder, divided
- 2 teaspoons baking powder
- ¼ teaspoon salt
- ½ cup rice milk
- 6 tablespoons dairy-free soy-free margarine, melted
- 1 teaspoon vanilla
- ⅔ cup packed dark brown sugar
- 1¼ cups hot water
- Dairy-free ice cream* (optional)

While there are quite a few dairy-free ice creams, many do contain soy, coconut or other allergens. Check labels.

1. Preheat oven to 350°F. Spray 8-inch square nonstick baking pan with nonstick cooking spray. Combine ¾ cup granulated sugar, flour, ¼ cup cocoa, baking powder and salt in large bowl. Beat in rice milk, margarine and vanilla. Spoon batter into prepared pan.

2. Combine remaining ¼ cup granulated sugar, ¼ cup cocoa and brown sugar in small bowl; mix well. Sprinkle mixture evenly over batter. Carefully pour hot water over batter. Do not stir.

3. Immediately place pan in oven. Bake 25 to 35 minutes or until cake quivers slightly when gently shaken. Remove from oven; let stand 15 minutes. Scoop into serving dishes. If desired, top each serving with dairy-free ice cream.   *Makes 8 servings*

marble sheet cake

free from

9 teaspoons powdered egg replacer, divided (equal to 6 eggs)
1⅓ cups plus 4 tablespoons water, divided
1 package (15 ounces) gluten-free yellow cake mix
1 cup (2 sticks) dairy-free margarine, softened, divided
2 teaspoons vanilla
1 package (15 ounces) gluten-free chocolate or devil's food cake mix
Creamy White Frosting (recipe follows)
Gluten-free chocolate sprinkles or other decorations

1. Preheat oven to 350°F. Spray 13×9-inch baking pan with nonstick cooking spray. Combine 4½ teaspoons powdered egg replacer and 2 tablespoons water in small bowl. Stir well. Combine remaining 4½ teaspoons egg replacer and 2 tablespoons water in another small bowl; stir well.

2. Combine yellow cake mix, ½ cup (1 stick) margarine, ⅔ cup water, one bowl of egg replacer mixture and vanilla in large bowl. Beat with electric mixer at low speed 30 seconds or until combined. Beat at medium speed 2 minutes or until smooth.

3. Combine chocolate cake mix, remaining ½ cup margarine, 1 cup water and remaining egg replacer mixture in large bowl. Beat with electric mixer at low speed 30 seconds or until combined. Beat at medium speed 2 minutes or until smooth.

4. Spoon yellow cake batter and chocolate cake batter alternately into prepared pan. Swirl together in zigzag pattern with knife or spatula for marble effect. Bake 40 to 50 minutes or until toothpick inserted into center comes out almost clean. Cool on wire rack.

5. Meanwhile prepare Creamy White Frosting. Frost and decorate cake as desired.

Makes 16 to 24 servings

creamy white frosting: Beat 4 ounces dairy-free cream cheese alternative and 3 tablespoons dairy-free margarine in medium bowl with electric mixer at medium speed until light and fluffy. Beat in 1½ teaspoons vanilla. Gradually beat in 4 cups powdered sugar. Beat in 4 to 6 tablespoons soymilk by tablespoonfuls until spreadable.

flower power strawberry cake

1 package (15 ounces) gluten-free yellow cake mix
1 container (6 ounces) strawberry soy yogurt
3 eggs
⅓ cup vegetable oil
1 package (4-serving size) strawberry gelatin
1 container prepared dairy-free vanilla frosting or
      Creamy White Frosting (page 136)
10 medium strawberries

1. Preheat oven to 350°F. Lightly grease 9-inch square baking pan.

2. Beat cake mix, yogurt, eggs, oil and gelatin in large bowl with electric mixer at low speed about 1 minute or until blended. Increase speed to medium; beat 1 to 2 minutes or until smooth. Spread batter in prepared pan.

3. Bake 38 to 43 minutes or until toothpick inserted into center comes out clean. Cool completely in pan on wire rack.

4. Frost and decorate with strawberry wedges to make flowers as shown in photo.

Makes 12 servings

Metric Conversion Chart

VOLUME MEASUREMENTS (dry)

¹/₈ teaspoon = 0.5 mL
¹/₄ teaspoon = 1 mL
¹/₂ teaspoon = 2 mL
³/₄ teaspoon = 4 mL
1 teaspoon = 5 mL
1 tablespoon = 15 mL
2 tablespoons = 30 mL
¹/₄ cup = 60 mL
¹/₃ cup = 75 mL
¹/₂ cup = 125 mL
²/₃ cup = 150 mL
³/₄ cup = 175 mL
1 cup = 250 mL
2 cups = 1 pint = 500 mL
3 cups = 750 mL
4 cups = 1 quart = 1 L

VOLUME MEASUREMENTS (fluid)

1 fluid ounce (2 tablespoons) = 30 mL
4 fluid ounces (¹/₂ cup) = 125 mL
8 fluid ounces (1 cup) = 250 mL
12 fluid ounces (1¹/₂ cups) = 375 mL
16 fluid ounces (2 cups) = 500 mL

WEIGHTS (mass)

¹/₂ ounce = 15 g
1 ounce = 30 g
3 ounces = 90 g
4 ounces = 120 g
8 ounces = 225 g
10 ounces = 285 g
12 ounces = 360 g
16 ounces = 1 pound = 450 g

DIMENSIONS

¹/₁₆ inch = 2 mm
¹/₈ inch = 3 mm
¹/₄ inch = 6 mm
¹/₂ inch = 1.5 cm
³/₄ inch = 2 cm
1 inch = 2.5 cm

OVEN TEMPERATURES

250°F = 120°C
275°F = 140°C
300°F = 150°C
325°F = 160°C
350°F = 180°C
375°F = 190°C
400°F = 200°C
425°F = 220°C
450°F = 230°C

BAKING PAN SIZES

Utensil	Size in Inches/Quarts	Metric Volume	Size in Centimeters
Baking or Cake Pan (square or rectangular)	8× 8× 2	2 L	20× 20× 5
	9× 9× 2	2.5 L	23× 23× 5
	12× 8× 2	3 L	30× 20× 5
	13× 9× 2	3.5 L	33× 23× 5
Loaf Pan	8× 4× 3	1.5 L	20× 10× 7
	9× 5× 3	2 L	23× 13× 7
Round Layer Cake Pan	8× 1½	1.2 L	20× 4
	9× 1½	1.5 L	23× 4
Pie Plate	8× 1¼	750 mL	20× 3
	9× 1¼	1 L	23× 3
Baking Dish or Casserole	1 quart	1 L	—
	1½ quart	1.5 L	—
	2 quart	2 L	—